Much of Venus is covered with lava

Venus

Steve Potts

A+

Smart Apple Media

COPYRIGHT

✳ Published by Smart Apple Media

1980 Lookout Drive, North Mankato, MN 56003

Designed by Rita Marshall

Copyright © 2002 Smart Apple Media. International copyright reserved in

all countries. No part of this book may be reproduced in any form without

written permission from the publisher.

Printed in the United States of America

✳ Photographs by Tom Stack & Associates (JPL, NASA, TSADO)

✳ Library of Congress Cataloging-in-Publication Data

Potts, Steve. Venus / by Steve Potts. p. cm. — (Our solar system series)

Includes bibliographical references and index.

✳ ISBN 1-58340-094-X

1. Venus (Planet)—Juvenile literature. [1. Venus (Planet)] I. Title.

QB621 .P68 2001   523.42—dc21   2001020124

✳   9 8 7 6 5 4 3 2 1

Venus

CONTENTS

Jewel of the Sky

In Roman mythology, Venus was the goddess of love. She was breathtaking to see. One of the most beautiful planets in our solar system is named for Venus. In fact, **Venus' day is 243 Earth days long; its year is 224.7 Earth days long.** Venus shines so brightly and beautifully that it has been called the "jewel of the sky." Venus appears in the morning sky just before the Sun rises. Venus also appears in the early evening, when it seems to follow the Sun as it sets. Because Venus appears

Venus is part of the huge Milky Way galaxy

in both the morning and night sky, some ancient peoples

thought Venus was actually two different planets. Because they

worshipped the Sun, they thought Venus was also very special.

Early Exploration

Early astronomers used the **telescope** to learn more

about Venus. In the 1600s, Galileo Galilei discovered that

Venus, like Earth's Moon, has phases. Phases occur when the

Sun lights different parts of a planet or moon's surface. As the

planet or moon moves through each phase, its shape seems to

change. Galileo and other early astronomers also found

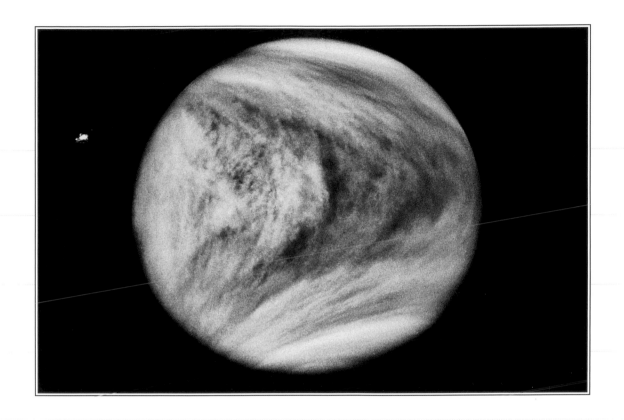

that Venus was covered by a thick layer of clouds. Sunlight

bounced off these clouds and gave Venus a bright color. These

clouds also blocked the surface of Venus from the astronomers'

Thick clouds hide Venus' surface from view

One of many active volcanoes on Venus

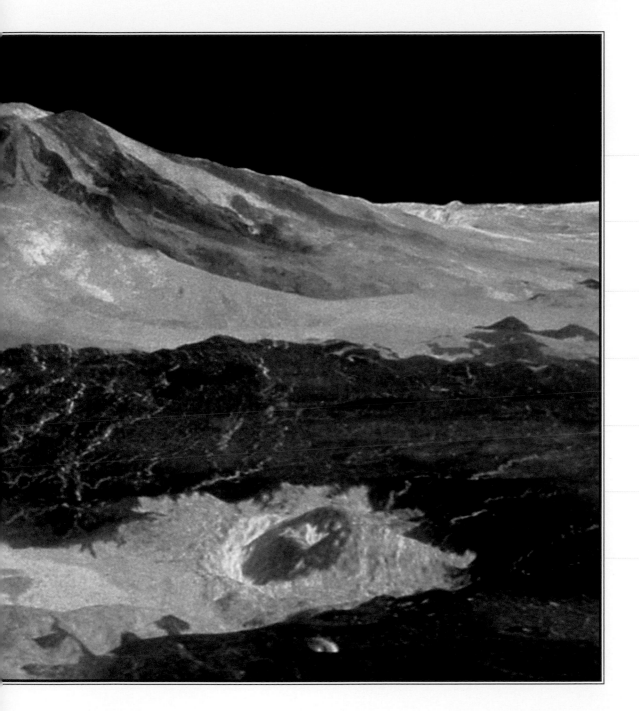

view. Until modern science came along, people could only guess what lay beneath the thick clouds covering Venus.

About Venus

Venus is the second planet from the Sun and is nearly the same size as Earth. But the similarities end there. For one thing, Venus rotates on its **axis** in the opposite direction that Earth rotates. On Earth, the Sun rises in the east and sets in the west. On Venus, however, the Sun rises in the west and sets in the east. ☀ From the surface of Venus, the stars are not visible through the clouds. The planet's atmosphere is about 96

percent carbon dioxide. It also contains sulphuric acid and

sulphur dust from volcanoes. The mixture of carbon dioxide

and sulphuric acid would kill humans if they tried to breathe

The nine planets of our solar system

it. ☀ Venus still has more than 1,000 active volcanoes, some more than 100 miles (160 km) in diameter. The lava from these volcanoes covers most of the planet's surface. ☀ The surface is also covered with craters left by meteorites. Many meteorites also strike Earth's atmosphere, but most of them break down into small pieces before they hit Earth.

The average surface temperature of Venus is 860° F (460° C).

On Venus, though, more than 900 craters cover the planet surface. These craters are huge, stretching from 1 mile (.6 km) to more than 100 miles (160 km) across. ☀ Astronomers have

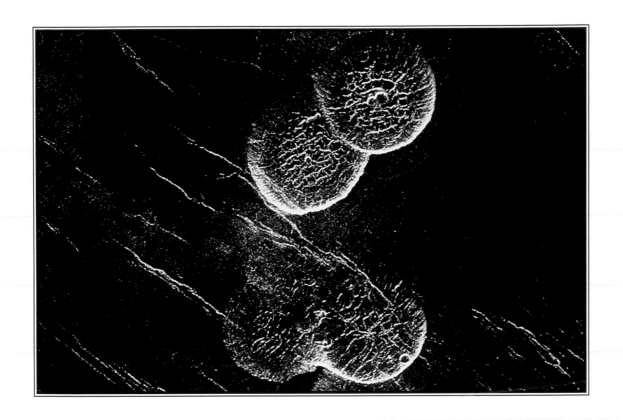

also found that the huge clouds over Venus move around the

planet at rapid speeds of more than 200 miles (320 km) per

hour. Because Venus is close to the Sun, the Sun's rays heat the

Venus' surface is dotted with lava domes

clouds above it. This causes the wind to blow so fiercely that the clouds move around the planet in just four or five days. Strangely, there are few winds close to the planet's surface.

Studying Venus

Because it is difficult to see Venus through its clouds, astronomers have been excited about using space probes to investigate the planet's atmosphere and surface. Probes are small spacecraft that are sent into space by rockets or are carried on a space shuttle. These probes carry complex com-

Lava domes average 15 miles (24 km) in diameter

puter and photographic equipment. The cameras take pictures

to send back to Earth by **radio waves**. ☀ The first probe

to visit Venus was *Mariner 2*, which flew by the planet in 1962.

In 1967, Russian probes began **orbiting** and landing on

Venus. In 1990, the American probe *Magellan* began mapping

the planet's surface. Most of what we know about Venus came

from information these probes gathered. ☀ There is no

evidence of water on Venus. The planet **Ancient astronomers called Venus the "morning star" and the "evening star."**

may have had water at one time, but it has

since evaporated in the hot temperatures.

Probes also have found no life in the harsh

conditions. Photographs taken by a probe in 1975 show a

landscape much like a desert. ☀ Scientists believe that

The unmanned *Magellan* space probe

studying Venus can help us learn more about other planets in

our solar system. The *Cassini* orbiter, a probe launched in 1997,

will pass by Venus twice before it heads out toward Saturn.

Cassini's photographs and other information will help

astronomers better understand the "jewel of the sky."

Venus' hot, desert-like surface

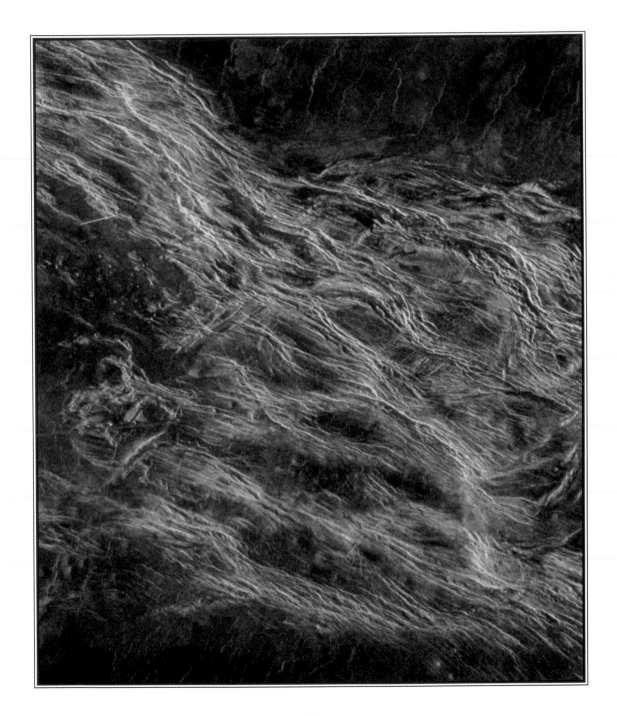

One of Venus' huge craters

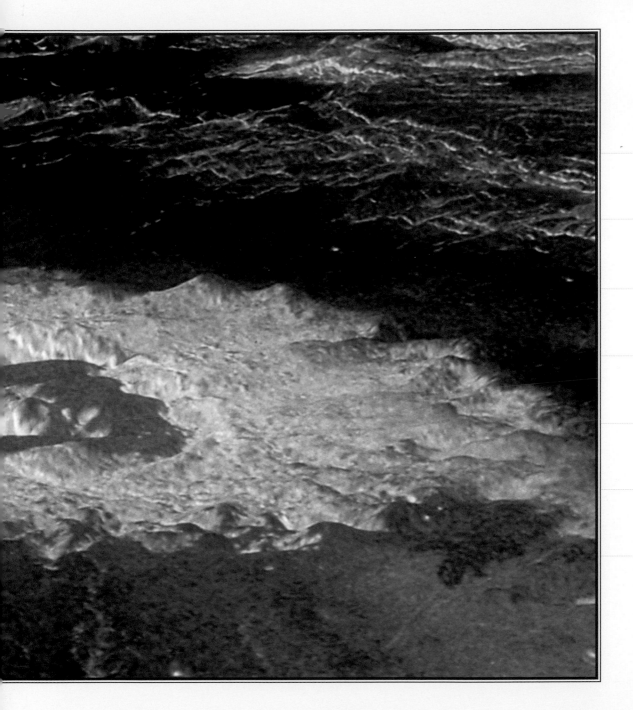

INFORMATION

Index

Words to Know

axis—a non-moving, imaginary line that an object rotates around

meteorites—pieces of rock and dust from outer space that fall to a planet's surface

orbiting—traveling in a repeating circular pattern around another object

radio waves—energy that travels at the speed of light from a transmitting antenna to a receiving antenna to form a message

telescope—an instrument that uses a glass lens to magnify distant objects

Read More

Bond, Peter. *DK Guide to Space*. New York: DK Publishing, 1999.

Couper, Heather, and Nigel Henbest. *DK Space Encyclopedia*. New York: DK Publishing, 1999.

Furniss, Tim. *Atlas of Space Exploration*. Milwaukee, Wisc.: Gareth Stevens Publishing, 2000.

Internet Sites

Astronomy.com
http://www.astronomy.com/home.asp

NASA: Just for Kids
http://www.nasa.gov/kids.html

Windows to the Universe
http://windows.engin.umich.edu/

The Nine Planets
http://seds.lpl.arizona.edu/nineplanets/nineplanets/